HOW TO BE A "POOP" DETECTIVE

Kristin Struble, MD, FAAP

Illustrated by Don Sidle

HOW TO BE A "POOP" DETECTIVE
by Kristin Struble, MD, FAAP

Published by
Dr. Bubbles, LLC

Illustrations: Don Sidle, DonSidle.net
Layout: Nick Zelinger, NZGraphics.com
Book Consultant: Judith Briles, The Book Shepherd
ISBN: 978-0-9969472-0-6 (hard cover)
ISBN: 978-0-9969472-1-3 (soft cover)
ISBN: 978-0-9969472-2-0 (eBook)

Library of Congress Cataloging in Publication Data on File

First Edition

Printed in the U.S.A.

In dedication to my mentors at Phoenix Children's Hospital and Maricopa Integrated Health Systems where I completed my pediatric specialty training and developed my commitment to the practice of pediatric medicine. I am blessed and honored to be associated with the caliber of physicians, nurses and ancillary clinicians at these caring and committed institutions.

I also offer special dedications to my family and friends for their continual support through this process.

I especially thank my husband, Steve, and my precious son, Luke. I truly cherish their patience and support as I incessantly spoke and continue to speak about my passions.

Finally, I dedicate this book to God, for without Him I could not be who I am.

Would you like to become a Poop Detective? Become one and you can smile and laugh out loud with "poop talk" and look for funny clues.

Guess what? This might sound silly and make you giggle, but your poop comes from what you eat and so do your toots.

Grandpas, grandmas, moms and dads, big sisters and baby brothers, they all toot and poop. If you teach them what you learn today, they'll be healthier and happier, just like you.

To be a good Poop Detective, you must learn five clues for healthy "poop." If you remember the five "S's", you will know what to do.

The 5 S's

1. SHAPE Its SHAPE should be like soft snakes, logs or even hot dog poops.

Not like eggs, baseballs, small nuggets, oatmeal or wet, slimy soup.

2. SOFT It should be SOFT and skinny.

3. SINK It should SINK to the bottom of the bowl!

4. SHADE Its SHADE should be brown.

5. SHOOT It should SHOOT out easy and fast every day. That is your goal.

The food you swallow moves through your pipe and all the way down. If it's healthy, it poops poop smoothly and comes out looking brown.

From that food, your body's pipe absorbs
all the vitamins you need to grow.
What's left is pushed on through the pipe
and comes out down below.

So always tell your parents if something's
wrong when you look into the bowl.
Remember, to be a good Poop Detective,
you must always stay on poop patrol.

Poop tells your body and brain the story of what you've put into your mouth.
Is it yelling out for help: "I'm stuck and can't find my way out 'south'!?"

Or possibly, instead, "My tummy hurts and I'm much too mushy and greasy."
Instead of saying, "I'm really all right; I'm moving so nice and easy."

So, when you poop, is there pain down there,
before it finally plopped?
Or did you yell, "Mom, come in here ... my poop's
running ... or has really stopped!"

Is your poop trying to tell you something,
you don't really want to know?
Like, "Hey, Poop Detective, the junk you ate
last night is now putting on a show."

Are you having tummy trouble?
Are you and it in a funk?
Are you bending over double
because you ate or drank some junk?

It's time to look for food-eating clues, as all good Poop Detectives do. Stop eating and drinking the garbage, that is messing up your poo!

A good Poop Detective asks himself,
"When and what did I last eat or drink?
Was it the milk or was it the cheese?
What is really making me stink?"

Hey Stinky! Wake up out there...

THINK! THINK! THINK!

Your pipe is warning you ..."Be on full alert! There's something you put into your mouth that made your body hurt."

As a Poop Detective, stop eating the food
you think is bad, just for a little while.
If that stops the trouble, before you know
it, you will be dancing with a great big smile.

Then bring back that food a little at a time,
to give you a knowing clue.
You might truly have solved the mystery of
the very thing that's been bugging you.

Remember, cow's milk and other animal's milk can give your tummy trouble.
As it moves and grooves on through your pipe, it makes your pipeline bubble!

Try a different kind of milk, one that's made
from different things.
Like almonds and rice and coconut milk; they'll
make your body sing!

Now you're getting smarter; remember to
practice what you learn.
Healthy, perfect poop should slide right
out and never sting or burn.

Try to get your snakes, submarines or logs
out smooth, each and every day.
As a Poop Detective, always look for clues,
you'll always find a way.

Healthy foods like fruits and greens will
keep your pipes in check.
When you eat sweets, drink cow's milk, soda
and juices, you'll soon become a wreck!

Our brain's a great detective. It knows your inner story.
It tells your body what it needs and keeps a full inventory.

Your doctor measures your every inch
to check how fast you're growing.
If everything's groovin' really well, you
and your parents will be glowing.

WAKE UP! YUMMY!

Breakfast is the best time for fruits. They really get you movin'.
Vegetables both for lunch and dinner, keep your pipeline groovin'.

Remember, instead of milk, drink water with every meal.
It rinses your every organ and improves the way you feel.

The 5 S's

1. Shape 2. Soft
3. Sink 4. Shade
5. Shoot

1. SHAPE Its SHAPE should be like soft snakes, logs or even hot dog poops.

2. SOFT It should be SOFT and skinny.

3. SINK It should SINK to the bottom of the bowl!

4. SHADE Its SHADE should be brown.

5. SHOOT It should SHOOT out easy and fast every day. That is your goal.

Always remember those five "S's"; they're
your clues to healthy poops.
Be sure to count on them; they'll always
help you stay in the right poop loop.

SUPER COOL!

If its SHAPE is like a brown-SHADED snake, is ... SOFT and
SINKABLE ... and SHOOTS out,
Then ... super cool ... is how you will feel ... each and every day!

DRAW ME!

Watch your "poop pictures" change as you change your diet!

DRAW ME!

DRAW ME!

DRAW ME!

About the Author

Kristin Struble, MD, FAAP is a practicing pediatrician in Phoenix, Arizona, since 2001. She was raised in Tucson, Arizona, and received her undergraduate degree at the University of Arizona in Nutritional Sciences. Inspired by her maternal grandfather, she went on to complete her postgraduate Medical Doctor degree at the University of Arizona College of Medicine, followed by a Pediatric residency at Phoenix Children's Hospital and Maricopa Integrated Health Systems.

Kristin is passionate about nutritional education, particularly in changing the traditional thinking of where children's calorie sources should come. Her attempt is to redefine "healthful calories" versus empty calories for parents as a simple tool in a lifelong journey for rearing a healthy child.

She is dedicated to promoting the message that a healthy diet is the best medicine and that the body talks to us through our poop. She wrote this book hoping to empower many more parents and changing the course of a child's life through these simple messages.

Raised by her parents Jake and Carol and surrounded by five siblings, Kristin learned the art of eating healthy firsthand. Dr. Struble is married to Stephen Chakmakian, DO, and has one precious son, Luke.

Her website is: www.kristinstruble.com.

About the Artist

Don Sidle is a cartoonist, designer and illustrator. He lives with his wife Jamie and two dogs Trip and Mokie in Denver, Colorado. He is a member of the Association of American Editorial Cartoonists and loves to draw.

REMEMBER:
Shape, Soft, Sink, Shade, Shoot!

DON'T MISS

the parent companion book

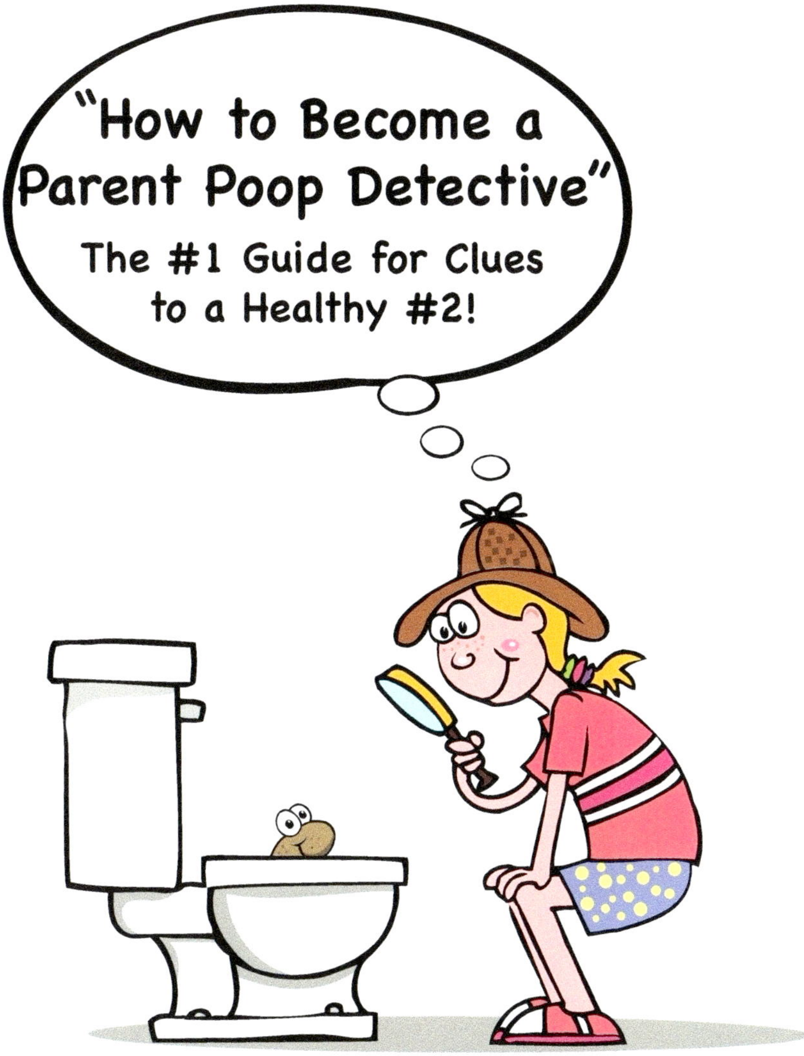